A GIFT

FOR: ....

FROM: ....

THE
Gift

UNWRAP THE MEANING
— *of the* —
CHRISTMAS SEASON

JOYCE MEYER

CONTENTS

O holy night,

the stars are brightly shining;

JESUS, LIGHT OF THE WORLD

Because of and through the heart of tender mercy and loving-kindness of our God, a Light from on high will dawn upon us and visit [us] to shine upon and give light to those who sit in darkness and in the shadow of death, to direct and guide our feet in a straight line into the way of peace.

LUKE 1:78-79

CHRISTMAS IS A BEAUTIFUL AND AMAZING TIME *of* THE YEAR.

It is a time to celebrate the birth of Christ. One of the ways we do that is by giving and receiving gifts, and as we do, it reminds us that Jesus is the greatest gift of all. Pure giving is one of the most beautiful things that we do, and I always encourage people to make every day Christmas as far as giving is concerned. Let's live in the spirit of Christmas all year round! *For God so loved the world that He gave*

His only begotten Son, that whoever believes in Him should not perish but have everlasting life (John 3:16 NKJV).

He is the light of the world (see John 8:12). If you just open up your eyes and look around, you can see that it's true. There is nothing that lights a person up like Jesus. He puts so much joy in your soul! Without Jesus, we would have no love or compassion to share with others. But because He lives in us, we can shine the light of His love throughout the entire world. That is the purpose God has for us.

First Peter 2:9 says we are a "chosen race" and a "royal priesthood," made to display the virtues and perfections of God, Who calls us out of darkness and into His marvelous light.

In other words, He has chosen you to shine His light in the world. It's very encouraging to know God doesn't expect us to be perfect before His love and light can shine through our lives. In fact, He chooses to work through "[frail, human] vessels of earth" (see 2 Corinthians 4:7).

You could say that you and I are like cracked pots. We will always have weaknesses and imperfections, but we never have to hide them from God. He loves us just the way we are! And His strength is made perfect in our weaknesses (see 2 Corinthians 12:9). As we open up our hearts to Him—exposing everything to the light of His love—He takes care of our cracks, flaws and weaknesses.

I love 2 Corinthians 3:18 because it is an incredible promise from God. It says that our lives are constantly being transformed into His image *in ever-increasing splendor* from one degree of glory to another. What an amazing gift!

The light of God actually intensifies in us as we allow Him to work in us and through us. And there are so many ways to shine His light. It can be as simple as wearing a smile.

As you go about your daily life—especially during this special season of celebration—I encourage you to set aside a portion of your time, energy, talents and resources to share that light and serve others. After all, this is what Christmas is really all about. Just as Jesus came to love and serve all of us by giving the greatest gift—His very life—we can give of ourselves because His life and light is in us. He is Emmanuel, God with us!

It is the night

of the dear Savior's birth!

Emmanuel, God with Us

Behold, a virgin shall be with child, and shall bring forth a son, and they shall call his name Emmanuel, which being interpreted is, God with us.

MATTHEW 1:23 KJV

GOD HAS A BEAUTIFUL PLAN FOR YOUR LIFE.

And He wants to lead you each step of the way. That is why one of the names of God, Emmanuel, means, "God with us." He wants to be intimately involved in our lives—to know His voice and follow Him.

In fact, He wanted to be with us so strongly that He sent His Son, a part of Himself, to physically walk the earth. That baby in the manger was God and He is still with us today.

When I think about the person I am today, I am amazed how God has changed me—and I'm so grateful for the ways He allows me to help others now.

There were times when I came very close to giving up along the way. But God was faithful to be with me, helping me and keeping me going on those days. I know that apart from Him, I can do nothing, and in Him, I have everything I need to live the abundant life He gives me in Christ.

It is the same for you. You can all have the strength and confidence to keep going because of what Jesus has done for *you*, because God is with you every day.

Have you noticed that when God speaks to your heart, He only has caring and encouraging things to say? He never asks us, "Why aren't you more like this person?"

or "When are you ever going to amount to something?" That's because in Christ, God sees you as perfect.

Many people don't realize God sees them that way. In fact, if you have ever been hurt or rejected, you may have thought that God is mad at you and doesn't really listen to your prayers. But that is not true. The reason we have Christmas is proof of that. Jesus came, He lived, He died, and He rose again so we can have real relationship with God.

God loves His children *unconditionally*. In Christ, you are His own special child.

Ephesians 1:5 says that God decided to adopt you because it gave Him great pleasure (NLT). You can't earn or buy His love. It is simply a gift He wants you to receive because you are so dear to Him—you are His child!

Romans 8:35-39 tells us that God loves us because He

wants to, and nothing in creation can separate us from His love. I encourage you to be bold enough to believe that God let Jesus come to earth and go through everything He went through just for you—because you're that precious and that valuable to Him.

Let this be God's Christmas gift to you: Take a step of faith and believe that God loves you intimately, He has a great plan for your life, and His promises are true.

He is always with you and He is truly the One who lights you up on the inside. As you turn the page to the Christmas story that is beautifully recorded in Luke chapter two, let the miracle of Jesus' coming—and what Christ, the Savior, did for you—sink deeper into your heart than ever before.

AND this shall be a sign unto you;

Ye shall find
the babe wrapped in
swaddling clothes,
lying in a manger.

THE CHRIST

MAS STORY

THE CHRISTMAS STORY FROM LUKE 2

A

¹AND IT CAME TO PASS IN THOSE DAYS, THAT THERE WENT OUT A DECREE *from* CAESAR AUGUSTUS that all the world should be taxed. 2 (And this taxing was first made when Cyrenius was governor of Syria.) 3 And all went to be taxed, every one into his own city. 4 And Joseph also went up from Galilee, out of the city of Nazareth, into Judaea, unto the city of David, which is called Bethlehem; (because he was of the house and lineage of David:) 5 To be taxed with Mary his espoused wife, being great with child. 6 And so it was, that, while they were there, the days were accomplished that she should be delivered. 7 **And she brought forth her firstborn son, and wrapped him in swaddling clothes, and laid him in a manger; because there was no room for them in the inn.**

8 And there were in the same country shepherds abiding in the field, keeping watch over their flock by night. 9 **And, lo, the angel of the Lord came upon them, and the glory of the Lord shone round about them: and they were**

sore afraid. 10 And the angel said unto them, Fear not: for, behold, I bring you good tidings of great joy, which shall be to all people. 11 **For unto you is born this day in the city of David a Saviour, which is Christ the Lord.** 12 And this shall be a sign unto you; Ye shall find the babe wrapped in swaddling clothes, lying in a manger.

13 **And suddenly there was with the angel a multitude of the heavenly host prais-** **ing God, and saying,** 14 **Glory to God in the highest, and on earth peace, good will toward men.**

15 And it came to pass, as the angels were gone away from them into heaven, the shepherds said one to another, Let us now go even unto Bethlehem, and see this thing which is come to pass, which the Lord hath made known unto us. 16 And they came with haste, and found Mary, and Joseph, and the babe

lying in a manger. 17 And when they had seen it, they made known abroad the saying which was told them concerning this child. 18 And all they that heard it wondered at those things which were told them by the shepherds. 19 But Mary kept all these things, and pondered them in her heart. 20 And the shepherds returned, glorifying and praising God for all the things that they had heard and seen, as it was told unto them.

21...HIS NAME WAS CALLED JESUS.

LUKE 2:1-21 KJV

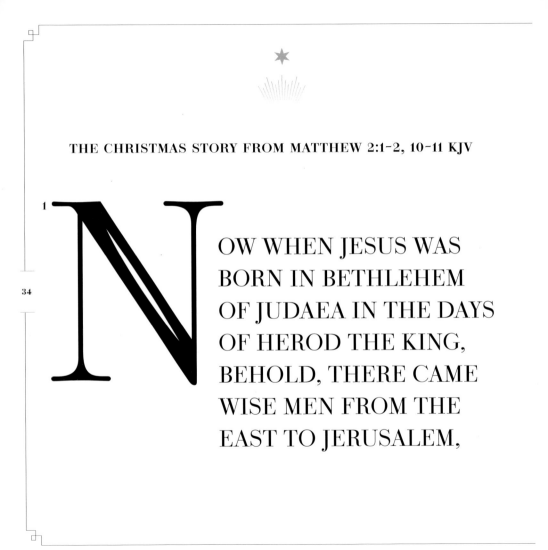

THE CHRISTMAS STORY FROM MATTHEW 2:1-2, 10-11 KJV

1 NOW WHEN JESUS WAS BORN IN BETHLEHEM OF JUDAEA IN THE DAYS OF HEROD THE KING, BEHOLD, THERE CAME WISE MEN FROM THE EAST TO JERUSALEM,

2 Saying, Where is he that is born King of the Jews? for we have seen his star in the east, and are come to worship him...

10 **When they saw the star, they rejoiced with exceeding great joy.**

11 And when they were come into the house, they saw the young child with Mary his mother, and fell down, and worshipped him: and when they had opened their treasures, they presented unto him gifts; gold, and frankincense and myrrh.

Joy to the world, the Lord is come!

Let earth receive her King

The Great I AM

For to us a child is born, to us a son is given, and the government will be on his shoulders. And he will be called Wonderful Counselor, Mighty God, Everlasting Father, Prince of Peace.

ISAIAH 9:6 NIV

JESUS WAS ALREADY IN HEAVEN BEFORE THE WORLD BEGAN— *a* FAR MORE GLORIOUS PLACE THAN YOU OR I CAN EVER IMAGINE.

Yet He chose to leave paradise so that one day, you and I can live eternally in the presence of God. Just let that soak in for a moment...

Because of all Jesus has done for us, Christmas is the perfect time to celebrate and sing about the miracle of His love, and how He came to rescue all mankind. And the way He came and how He lived as a man on this earth reveals so much to us about the true character of God and His amazing love for all of us.

That night in Bethlehem, our infant Savior was humbly laid in a simple bed of straw. As a boy, He played and studied in the modest household of a carpenter. As a man, Jesus lived His life as a perfect example, enduring every kind of earthly temptation—and then humbled Himself to the point of death on a cross.

Philippians 2:8-9 says that because Jesus humbled Himself to the extreme, God has highly exalted Him and has freely bestowed on Him the name that is above every name.

You and I now know Jesus not as a helpless infant or even a grown-up man, but the King of Kings, the Lord of Lords, *the Great I Am.* His greatness goes beyond what any one of us can fully comprehend.

There are many scriptures that show us what it means for God to be our "I AM."

I encourage you to pause here and consider the majesty of God, and the goodness and power He brings to your life. As you reflect on these things, you can truly begin to celebrate the miracle of His love. Having a close, personal relationship with Jesus is truly the greatest gift of all.

I Am the Light of the World
JOHN 9:5

I Am the Alpha and the Omega
REVELATION 1:8

I Am the Bread of Life
JOHN 6:35

I Am the Way and the Truth and the Life
JOHN 14:6

I Am the Good Shepherd
JOHN 10:11

I am the True Vine
JOHN 15:1

I Am the Bright Morning Star
REVELATION 22:16

Silent night, holy night,

Son of God, love's pure light

THE GREATEST GIFTS OF ALL

Let the little children come to me, and do not hinder them, for the kingdom of God belongs to such as these.

MARK 10:14 NIV

The moment you receive Christ as your Savior, you receive everything He is in your spirit. In and through Him, you are a joint heir of the Kingdom of God, which Romans 14:17 says is righteousness, peace and joy in the Holy Spirit. There is such power in those gifts! All you need to do to enjoy them is open your heart to God and receive them, like a child on Christmas morning. You don't even have to wait. You can start unwrapping His gifts right now!

PEACE

★

Peace I leave with you; My [own] peace I now give and bequeath to you. – JOHN 14:27

Jesus—the Prince of Peace—wants us to have *His* peace in every part of our lives, at all times. This verse goes on to say, *Do not let your hearts be troubled, neither let them be afraid.* Instead of hanging on to worry, anxiety, fear or frustration, you can receive His gift of supernatural peace. Moment by moment, day by day, I encourage you to put your trust in God. As you go through the process of releasing your worries and cares to Him, you will find a peace that surpasses all understanding.

UNWRAP PEACE

LET THE PEACE OF CHRIST RULE IN YOUR HEARTS, SINCE AS MEMBERS OF ONE BODY YOU WERE CALLED TO PEACE. AND BE THANKFUL.

Do not be anxious about anything, but in every situation, by prayer and petition, with thanksgiving, present your requests to God. And the peace of God, which transcends all understanding, will guard your hearts and your minds in Christ Jesus.

YOU WILL KEEP IN PERFECT PEACE THOSE WHOSE MINDS ARE STEADFAST, BECAUSE THEY TRUST IN YOU.

COLOSSIANS 3:15 NIV

PHILIPPIANS 4:6-7 NIV

ISAIAH 26:3 NIV

Radiant beams

from Thy holy face

THE GIFT OF

JOY

★

In Your presence is fullness of joy, at Your right hand there are pleasures forevermore. – PSALM 16:11

54

Fullness of joy is found not in God's presents, but in His *presence.* That's why the Bible says we can have inexpressible, glorious, triumphant, heavenly joy no matter what is happening around us. One of the easiest ways to increase your joy and the joy of others is to keep your heart and mind focused on God and His Word. As you carry out your daily responsibilities and activities, ask God to help you and lead you. Then relax in the overwhelming, empowering joy of the Lord—joy that cannot be fully explained or understood!

UNWRAP JOY

Nehemiah said,
"Go and enjoy choice
food and sweet drinks,
and send some to those
who have nothing
prepared. This day is
holy to our Lord.
Do not grieve, for the
joy of the Lord is
your strength."

THE LORD
HAS DONE
GREAT THINGS
FOR US,
AND WE ARE
FILLED WITH
JOY.

Those the Lord has
rescued will return.
They will enter
Zion with singing;
everlasting joy will
crown their heads.
Gladness and joy will
overtake them, and
sorrow and sighing
will flee away.

NEHEMIAH 8:10 NIV

PSALM 126:3 NIV

ISAIAH 51:11 NIV

RIGHTEOUSNESS

✶

God made him who had no sin to be sin for us, so that in him we might become the righteousness of God.

–2 CORINTHIANS 5:21 NIV

Righteousness is right standing with God. When we accept Jesus, He gives us the gift of His righteousness, and by faith, we are made right with God. You don't have to worry about making mistakes. God knows you will make them! But because of Jesus, you can rest in His righteousness. As you unwrap this incredible gift, pray with boldness. Remember, He doesn't hear or answer our prayers because we are good; He hears and answers because He is good!

UNWRAP RIGHTEOUSNESS

THE FRUIT OF THAT RIGHTEOUSNESS WILL BE PEACE; ITS EFFECT WILL BE QUIETNESS AND CONFIDENCE FOREVER.

ISAIAH 32:17 NIV

"For the eyes of the Lord are on the righteous and his ears are attentive to their prayer, but the face of the Lord is against those who do evil." Who is going to harm you if you are eager to do good? But even if you should suffer for what is right, you are blessed....

1 PETER 3:12-14 NIV

SURELY, LORD, YOU BLESS THE RIGHTEOUS; YOU SURROUND THEM WITH YOUR FAVOR AS WITH A SHIELD.

PSALM 5:12 NIV

With the dawn of redeeming grace

HOPE

✦

Our hope is certain. It is something for the soul to hold on to. It is strong and secure. – HEBREWS 6:19 NIRV

Hope is an extraordinary gift. It allows us to experience peace and joy as we simply believe God's Word and the promises it holds. Romans 15:13 says that by the power of the Holy Spirit, we can overflow or "bubble over" with hope. Although we can't prevent negative feelings from ever showing up, we can quickly chase them away by choosing hope-filled thoughts, words and actions. Our hope is in Christ and He will never fail us.

UNWRAP HOPE

Praise be to the God and Father of our Lord Jesus Christ! In his great mercy he has given us new birth into a living hope through the resurrection of Jesus Christ from the dead.

MAY THE GOD OF HOPE FILL YOU WITH ALL JOY AND PEACE AS YOU TRUST IN HIM, SO THAT YOU MAY OVER-FLOW WITH HOPE BY THE POWER OF THE HOLY SPIRIT.

And hope does not put us to shame, because God's love has been poured out into our hearts through the Holy Spirit, who has been given to us.

1 PETER 1:3 NIV

ROMANS 15:13 NIV

ROMANS 5:5 NIV

THE GIFT OF

FAITH

★

All of you are God's children because of your faith in Christ Jesus. — GALATIANS 3:26 CEV

Faith in God brings a supernatural rest into our souls, allowing us to live simply and freely, the way He wants us to live. Trust doesn't just happen in our relationship with God, but grows as we come to know Him more personally, take steps of faith and experience His faithfulness. It is a gift that is often released through the power of prayer and thanksgiving. I encourage you to ask God to help you develop a deeper trust in Him, and then thank Him in advance for the gift of faith He has given you.

UNWRAP FAITH

NOW FAITH IS CONFIDENCE IN WHAT WE HOPE FOR AND ASSURANCE ABOUT WHAT WE DO NOT SEE.

These have come so that the proven genuineness of your faith— of greater worth than gold, which perishes even though refined by fire— may result in praise, glory and honor when Jesus Christ is revealed.

FOR EVERYONE BORN OF GOD OVERCOMES THE WORLD. THIS IS THE VICTORY THAT HAS OVER- COME THE WORLD, EVEN OUR FAITH.

HEBREWS 11:1 NIV

1 PETER 1:7 NIV

1 JOHN 5:4 NIV

63

THE GIFT OF

LOVE

✦

**Three things will last forever—faith, hope, and love—
and the greatest of these is love.** – 1 CORINTHIANS 13:13 NLT

God's Word teaches us to love everyone, including ourselves.
As you receive God's love and begin to see yourself through
His eyes, then you will be able to love others the way God
loves them. God's love is a wondrous gift that He freely
gives us. We can't earn it and we don't deserve it, yet He
willingly and continually longs to express His love to us. All
we need to do is open our hearts, believe His Word, and receive it with thankfulness. Believe that God loves you with
an everlasting love, and then share that love with others.

UNWRAP LOVE

THE LORD APPEARED TO US IN THE PAST, SAYING: "I HAVE LOVED YOU WITH AN EVERLASTING LOVE; I HAVE DRAWN YOU WITH UNFAILING KINDNESS."

Love is patient, love is kind. It does not envy, it does not boast, it is not proud. It does not dishonor others, it is not self-seeking, it is not easily angered, it keeps no record of wrongs ... It always protects, always trusts, always hopes, always perseveres.

AND WALK IN THE WAY OF LOVE, JUST AS CHRIST LOVED US AND GAVE HIMSELF UP FOR US AS A FRAGRANT OFFERING AND SACRIFICE TO GOD.

65

JEREMIAH 31:3 NIV

1 CORINTHIANS 13:4-7 NIV

EPHESIANS 5:2 NIV

Jesus, Lord, at Thy birth,

Jesus, Lord, at Thy birth.

THERE IS SO MUCH MORE *to* UNWRAP!

The Christmas story is the place where we begin our journey with Christ through a personal relationship with Him. But it's just a beginning. John 10:10 says that Jesus came so we *may have and enjoy life, and have it in abundance (to the full, till it overflows.)* God is an abundant God, Who is greater than we can comprehend, and He has more for us than we know. We can never reach the end of who He is and what He offers us in Christ.

I want to encourage you to continue to pursue a deeper, more intimate relationship with Him through the Word and prayer each day. As you do, God will fill your heart with the peace and joy of Christmas the whole year through! Have a wonderful, amazing, holiday season.

Joyce

CHRISTMAS
CAROLS
to ENJOY

O HOLY NIGHT

1st Stanza

O holy night, the stars
are brightly shining;

It is the night of the dear
Savior's birth!

Long lay the world in sin
and error pining,

Till He appeared and the
soul felt its worth.

A thrill of hope, the weary
soul rejoices,

For yonder breaks a new
and glorious morn.

Fall on your knees, O hear
the angel voices!

O night divine, O night
when Christ was born!

O night divine, O night,
O night divine!

*"O Holy Night" Placide Cappeau (French, 1847);
translated to English by John S. Dwight (1855)*

★

SILENT NIGHT
3rd Stanza

Silent night, holy night,

Son of God, love's pure light;

Radiant beams from
Thy holy face

With the dawn of
redeeming grace,

Jesus, Lord, at Thy birth,

Jesus, Lord, at Thy birth.

Silent night, holy night

Wondrous star,
lend thy light;

With the angels let us sing,

Alleluia to our King;

Christ the Savior is born,

Christ the Savior is born!

*"Silent Night" Josef Mohr (German, circa 1816-1818);
translated to English by John F. Young (1863)*

★

JOY TO THE WORLD
1st and 2nd Stanza

Joy to the world,
the Lord is come!

Let earth receive her King;

Let every heart prepare
Him room,

And Heaven and nature sing,

And Heaven and nature sing,

And Heaven, and Heaven,
and nature sing.

Joy to the earth,
the Savior reigns!

Let men their songs employ;

While fields and floods,
rocks, hills and plains

Repeat the sounding joy,

Repeat the sounding joy,

Repeat, repeat,
the sounding joy.

"Joy to the World" Isaac Watts (1719)

Published by *Joyce Meyer Ministries*
P.O. Box 655
Fenton, Missouri 63026

Printed in USA
ISBN: 978-0-9772930-9-4